C000120820

AN A-Z of LOONEY LIMERICKS

(for big kids)

by

Bernie Morris

and

Linda Koperski

Published by Hometime Books in the
United Kingdom 2009

Text copyright Bernie Morris © 2000
excepting verses that are signed *Anonymous*
from unknown sources.
Illustration copyright Linda Koperski © 2008

Hometimebooks.co.uk

Introduction

Since my school days when I accidentally discovered this form of verse called 'Limerick', I have often wondered about the origin of the name. Was it invented in Ireland perhaps? After some research and several years, I think not. The limerick must have been invented long before it reached the jocular pubs of Limerick in Ireland where the Irish undoubtedly made very good use of it whilst consuming copious amounts of Guinness.

It was Edward Lear who created the original limerick, and is credited with *A Book of Nonsense* (1846). Apparently, he did this to amuse his clients' children while they were waiting for their parents' having portraits painted. Edward Lear was an artist first and a poet last. How strange then that we remember him mostly for limericks? Since writing many of these little jocular verses, I have noticed a strange effect that keeps you reading: each time you read one limerick, you just cannot help reading the next, especially when they are nicely set out on a page. I am particularly proud of my lim-sagas, of which only two are contained in this book, but I consider them the best of my collection.

It pains me to see how modern society has totally corrupted the limerick and given it the reputation of lewdness which, in turn, has morally barred our children from even taking a peek into this wonderful form of fun and rhythm. I think Edward Lear would turn in his grave if he knew that.
I have therefore decided to reinvent the limerick as it was originally intended: to poke fun, irreverence, just plain daftness, or erroneous behaviour.

This book is not intended for very young readers, but for anyone who is a 'big kid' at heart. I would suggest parental guidance for children under 13, as it contains slang, made-up words and some (very mild) strong language.
Please enjoy nevertheless...

Acknowledgements

To my publisher, Steven Julien, for his courage and total belief in new genres and unknown authors; to Linda for beautiful artwork; to Robert Morris and George Palmer for their technical support.
To Koi Quittenton for the Cancerian picture, when she was only 12, and to Barbara Tepper for poetical inspiration and contribution.

Contents

Alan's Salon

A dapper young fellow named Alan
Did run a fine hairdressing salon.
He curled lots of hair
With meticulous care,
And used up shampoo by the gallon.

Aaron

There was a young fellow named Aaron
Whose head didn't have any hair on.
He tried every cure
From mould to manure
But nothing would propagate thereon.

Alice in Wonderland

Such a very nice girl was our Alice,
She never bore anyone malice.
Her one greatest dream
Was to end up as Queen,
And mortgage the Buckingham Palace.

Annie's Granny

There was a young lady called Annie
Who had an incredible granny.
She poured the old dear
A big glass of beer
And the speed it went down was uncanny.

Aries Rush In

Aries, the very first sign
Is always at front of the line.
Impatient and brash,
All parties will crash
With copious amounts of red wine.

'Arry Amorous

There was a young spider called 'Arry
Who thought it was high time to marry.
    He combed all his hair
    With meticulous care
        Then winked till his eyes
                went all starry.

Arry in the Drink

    'Arry's a friendly young spider
    His smile couldn't get any wider.
But one time it faltered
And very much altered
      When he landed "plop" in the cider.

B

Back to Basics

A delinquent today is defined
As a kid to whom life was unkind.
But don't you agree
The problem might be
No-one ever dared smack his behind?

Anonymous

Bare Bones

A skeleton once known as Steve
Said, "Nobody comes here to grieve.
They're probably scoffin'
At me in my coffin;
If I had the guts, I would leave."

Anonymous

Barney's Feast

There was a young fellow named Barney
Who fancied a chilli-con-carne.
It turned out too hot,
But it wasn't a lot.
He finished up munching a sarnie.

Bearing Up *(when down)*

There was a young bear who would fly.
He was surely a true Gemini.
He donned a smart jacket
Which cost him a packet,
And said "What a cool bear am I."

But sadly his plane came to grief.
He escaped by the skin of his teeth.
He said "As a test pilot,
I'm one shrinking violet."
And sat there and shook like a leaf.

Beauty Secret

There once was a clever old maid
Who ate only grape marmalade.
At age ninety-three
She said, "Look at me;
How nicely preserved I have stayed."

Anonymous

Beethoven

Old Beethoven surely could boast
Of talent far greater than most;
His musical treats
Were magical feats
Because he was deaf as a post.

Anonymous

Betty Boo-Boo

There was a young lady called Betty
Who considered all rules to be petty.
She hired a fast boat
Which soon failed to float
And ended up rammed in a jetty.

Bronwyn

Bronwyn, the sheep debonair,
When invited by Wolf to his lair,
Politely did baa
And told him "No ta,
I've a prior engagement elsewhere."

Bill's Barmy Bird

A birdkeeper name of Bill Barratt
Possessed an ungainly young parrot.
One day with a lurch,
It fell off its perch,
Whilst trying to dismember a carrot.

Cancerian

The sign of the Crab is a pearl –
Cannot wait for her claws to uncurl.
She'll reach for the moon,
Then have babies – too soon.
What a lovely impossible girl!

Capricorn Style

Capricorn's fond of old bones
And also of whinges and moans.
He's very ambitious
But not at all vicious
And his lectures are classic 'sleep zones'.

Chris's Lament

There was a young man named Chris-topher
Who thought he would buy a pet gopher.
The first thing it did
Was bite him - then hid
For three days behind the old sofa.

Cinderella's Day

Cinders, unfortunate lass
Was bullied by sisters, quite crass.
Yet she went to the ball
And said, "xxxx" to them all,
Wearing chiffon and slippers of glass.

Clare, Unaware

There was a young lady called Clare
Who thought it was quite rude to stare;
But sadly, she found
By just watching the ground,
She missed everything, everywhere.

Carol's Chill

None felt the cold more than Carol
Who liked to wear lots of apparel.
Three dresses she wore
And coats, three or four,
Till she looked just as round as a barrel.

Crying 'Wolf!'

Matilda, we're told in a pome,
Told stories predestined to roam.
When she cried out, "Fire! Fire!"
The crowd shouted, "Liar!"
And left her to burn with her home.

Culinary Art

When the cannibals started their fires
To boil a Franciscan named Meyers,
The Chief told the cook,
"The recipe book
Says you don't boil Franciscans, they're friars."

Anonymous

Cyril's Company

A hungry young fellow named Cyril
Went off on a picnic to Wirral.
He sat on the ground
And spread food all around
Which was very soon nicked by a squirrel.

D

Dan Dino'

Dan was a fat dinosaur
Too heavy to get off the floor;
So he sat in a stream
Made of melted ice cream
And supped it all up through a straw.

Dana the Vain

An unfortunate lady called Dana
Just couldn't have been any plainer
Till she got a face lift
As a cool birthday gift
And then she grew very much vainer.

Dave's Folly

There was an old hermit called Dave
Who had lived all his life in a cave;
By the time he came out,
He was crippled with gout
And was bowled off his feet by a wave.

Dick's Kick

Dick Turpin, a highwayman bold,
Robbed many a stagecoach of gold
And from each outraged miss,
He would then steal a kiss
(Unless she were ugly or old).

Dennis the Menace

A kid with a red stripy top,
Whose hair was a spiky great mop,
Had a mad dog called Gnasher
Who was quite a dasher
And spanks he did frequently cop.

Dragon's Resolution

There once was an unruly dragon
Who liked to drink wine by the flagon.
By the time he'd had ten,
He saw little green men
And decided to go on the wagon.

Dry Run

Count Dracula let out a moan,
"I guess that I ought to have known...
(I sucked without gain
On Mick Jagger's vein)
'Cos you can't extract blood from a stone!"

Anonymous

Ealing Efforts

A talentless lady from Ealing
Was eager to paint her own ceiling.
She climbed up a ladder
Which was even sadder;
Her legs were much less than appealing.

Edie-Greedy

There was an old woman called Edie
Whose eyes were incredibly beady.
She took what she saw,
But wanted much more.
She was so insatiably greedy.

Egg 'n Chips

Take one hefty spud without eyes.
Peel this and cut lengths of slim size.
Cook these in deep oil
Which is likely to boil.
Do this while your egg gently fries.

Elvis

Elvis, the legend lives on,
Although indisputably gone.
He's now on CD
And we think you'll agree,
No-one since has so vividly shone.

Ernie's Journey

An adventurous fellow called Ernie
Decided to make a long journey,
But soon lost his way,
And to monsters fell prey
In a forest so tall, dark and ferny.

Euclidity

Euclid was quite good at sums.
He didn't need stones out of plums.
He wrote geomet-ry
For the whole world to see.
He knew that what goes up, down comes.

Eva's Tales

Such a great story-teller was Eva
That no-one could ever believe her.
She told such big lies,
You could only surmise
That your very own ears did deceive yer.

F

The Face that Launched...

Fair Helen of Troy was insane.
Concussion had addled her brain
From bashing her skull
Against a ship's hull.
Why waste any decent champagne?

Anonymous

Fair Fairy

There once was a gorgeous young fairy
Who thought it a shame to be lairy.
She vowed to be good
Whenever she could,
And not to grow ugly or hairy.

Flaunty

There was a young lady named Flora
Who wanted the world to adore her.
She tried to impress
With the style of her dress,
Yet most of the World did ignore her.

Fraidy-Cat

There was once a young fellow named Mark,
Who was frightened of trees in the dark.
A friend asked, "At night,
Do you think they will bite?"
He said, "No, I'm afraid of their bark."

Anonymous

Fred's Bed

There was a young fellow named Fred
Who just couldn't get out of bed.
Though he set his alarm
With never a qualm,
He slept on as if he were dead.

Frankly – Weird

There was an old chap name of Frankie
Who just couldn't stand hanky-panky.
He wanted to be
In a monaster-ee
But the Abbot just thought him too cranky.

French Cooking Lesson

"My omelettes are fluffy, not tough,"
Said Henri, the chef at Le Boeuf.
"I blend them with cheese;
They're light as a breeze,
And only one egg is un oeuf."
by Bluebird

Frog on the Rebound

A frog once a-wooing did go.
He was lonely if you want to know.
He'd auditioned for 'Bud'
And they'd called his voice 'crud',
So he kissed a frog princess called Flo'.

Fred the Red

An alien once known as Fred
Was tired of being green (so he said).
So he filled up a sink
With some dye that was pink,
Dived in and turned bright flaming **red**.

DYE

G

Gary the Merry

There was a young fellow called Gary
Who was just as happy as Larry.
He laughed all the time
And was ever sublime,
Until he was tempted to marry.

Gerald's Row

A flamboyant fellow called Gerald
Quite fancied himself as a herald.
His bugle he blew
Till his friends cried "Boo, Boo!"
And ended up somewhat imperilled.

Giant Problem

There once was a horrible giant
Who thought he was quite self-reliant.
He scared lots of folk
Each time that he spoke
But found they were mostly defiant.

Goblin's Travel

There once was an ugly old Goblin
Who just couldn't walk without hobblin',
So he bought a new bike
To save him a hike
And ended up weaving and wobblin'.

Ghostly Scare

There once was a silly old ghost
Who thought he could scare folk the most.
He haunted a house
Till he met a big mouse,
Then screeched and flew up a lamp-post.

Great Grannie

Great grand-kids are not two a penny.
Some people don't even have any.
But lucky old me,
I've got twenty-three –
It's my fault that there are so many!

Gummed-Up

Bubble-gum is my favourite chew.
I munch till it's just so much goo.
Then bubbles I blow
Just as big as they'll grow,
Till it splats on my face – Yucky-Boo!

Gus Stop

A slow-moving chappie called Gus
Just never quite could catch a bus.
Each time one retreated,
He felt so defeated,
Which caused him to swear and to cuss.

Glynnis' Tipple

A beautiful pussy named Glynnis
Was remarkably fond of draught Guinness.
She lapped from her bowl
With incredible soul
And tiddly she got with great finesse.

H

Hazel's Dilemma

Such a very shy lady was Hazel,
She just couldn't handle appraisal.
Her thoughts became scattered
Upon being flattered;
Her speech became notably nasal.

Helen the Felon

A light-fingered lady named Helen,
Had a passion for honeydew melon.
She could not pass a grove,
As hard as she strove.
Her weakness did make her a felon.

Hic!

Hickory Dickory Dock!
Miss Mouse didn't run up the clock,
For she'd heard of the fate
Of her last scaredy mate.
Who still suffered hiccups from shock.

Hilda's Choice

There was a nice lady called Hilda
Who thought an ice-cream might have chilled her;
So she ordered a chilli,
Which was rather silly,
So hot that it very near killed her.

Horror Story

Last night I was guest at the Schmidts'
I left there scared out of my wits;
There were hideous shrieks,
And pictures of freaks
And towels marked "His", "Hers" and "Its".

Anonymous

Humpty's Folly

Humpty's a silly old egg.
To stand on he had not a leg
And that's why he fell
Off the 'wall out of hell'.
He should have been fixed with a peg.

Hush-A-Bye

Hush-a-bye Baby we're told
Was bunged up a tree in the cold.
Now that wasn't fair,
P'raps his Mum didn't care –
Yet he gave us this lullaby old.

Heather's Mishap

There was a young lady named Heather
Who just couldn't stand windy weather.
One day in a storm
Which was worse than the norm,
She was gusted away like a feather.

I

Ice Queen

An icicle crown will enhance
Silver locks, like a wild blizzard dance.
With skin white as snow
And garments that flow;
Her cold eyes can freeze at a glance.

Iggy's Cheek

An unruly monk named Ignatius
Was known to be rather audacious.
To his long-suffering abbot
Said, "Father, this habit –
Is it not just a bit ostentatious?"

Ike's Catch

There was a young fellow named Ike
Who thought he would fish off a dyke.
The bait that he took
Was a frog on a hook
So he landed a great monster pike.

Irene's Tub

There was a young lady, I-rene,
Obsessed with remaining quite clean.
She bathed night and day,
Till her skin wore away
And the sides of the bath turned bright green.

Isis

There's a river in Oxford called Isis
Not known for its virtues or vices.
But with every boat race,
Its flow sets the pace
And sometimes results in a crisis.

Itchy

There was a young guy with an itch,
Who found it a bit of a bitch.
He scratched like a cat
And a wild one at that.
He must've been cursed by a witch.

Ivor's Talent

There was a young rocker named Ivor
Who was an incredible jiver.
He danced all night long
To each rock 'n roll song,
And drinks cost him only a fiver.

J

Jane's Laziness

There was a young lady called Jane
Who thought washing-up was a pain;
So she piled all her crocks
In a big cardboard box
And left them all out in the rain.

Jenny's Poverty

There was a poor lady named Jenny
And wealth she just didn't have any.
Whilst in a posh shop,
To the loo she did pop
And found she was short of a penny.

Jim's Diet

A very fat fellow named Jim
Just wanted to be very slim.
But after he tried it,
He couldn't abide it,
'Cos no-one could recognise him.

Jock's Anonymity

There was a young fellow named John
Who preferred to remain quite anon
So he signed all his cheques
With a wobbly great X
And soon all his money was gone.

Janet's Greed

A greedy young lady named Janet
Had an appetite much like a gannet.
She ate so much stuff
That was never enough;
Her waistline grew round as a planet.

Joe the Cave Man
(a Limsaga)

In the Stone Age, a long time ago,
Lived a cave-man, and his name was Joe.
He hunted and swore,
Went to parties galore,
But his spirit hung heavy with woe.

For he loved a sweet cave-girl called Bo,
But here's what was troubling Joe:
All the guys of the tribe
Brought her gifts as a bribe
In their efforts to make her heart glow.

Joe returned to his cave to decide
On a present that he could provide,
Like a much better prize
Which would outshine those guys',
And perhaps capture Bo for his bride.

He thought very hard and he frowned,
For thinking was not his home ground.
Then he suddenly roared,
(His old Mum was quite floored)
A perfect solution he'd found.

A plesiosaur-ass he'd find,
The colossalest one of its kind.
Sweet Bo could then feast
On this wonderful beast...
His Mum said, "You're outta your mind."

For no man had ever dared yet
So monstrous a creature to get.
"You'll get mangled for sure,
Or be drowned in manure..."
But Joe said,   "Do you wanna bet?"

He selected a huge mammoth bone
(Which was better than slinging a stone);
Then, with this mighty club
And a sackful of grub,
He embarked on his venture alone.

The Plessy, he knew, could be found,
In a lake that was dark and profound.
When Joe arrived weary,
The silence was eerie,
Unruffled, with nary a sound.

Old Plessy was sleeping, no doubt,
From his feeding exertions worn out,
On the bed of the lake.
Now to get him awake,
Joe would need to do more than just shout.

By the lake stood a very tall tree,
Which was laden with fruit heavily.
Joe climbed up the trunk
(Easy work for a hunk),
And began to throw fruits – one-two-three.

Plop, plop, in the lake went each fruit.
Joe hoped this would wake up the brute.
When the beast's head appeared,
He felt mightily cheered;
His joy was intensely acute.

Plessy ate all the fruit to be found
Then he eagerly looked all around,
In a search for some more.
Then the cave-man he saw,
And emitted a loud belching sound.

Now, Plessy was no carnivore,
A run-of-the-mill dinosaur.
But woe if he sat on you,
Farted or spat on you –
Then, you'd be truly done-for.

Two great golden eyes stared at Joe
In a small head that swayed to and fro,
On a neck that was long.
And a terrible pong
Arose from its breath with each blow.

Joe nearly fell out of his tree,
Alarmed by this close scrutiny,
But he kept very still
With an effort of will,
And stayed just as calm as could be.

Joe needed to find a new tack
To hasten his monster attack.
So he hurled a large fruit
Way, way past the dumb brute,
Who turned to go after the snack.

After Plesiosaur-ass had swerved,
To capture the treat that was served,
Joe leaped on its back
For a final attack
And Plessy became quite unnerved.

Old Plessy then started to bellow.
No longer was he feeling mellow.
He bucked and he thrashed
And he heaved, and he splashed,
Attempting to shake off this fellow.

Joe had to hang on rather grimly;
His senses were reeling quite dimly.
He raised his great bone
With a bit of a groan
And aimed at the head,
        rather primly.

PAF!

CRACK...

Mammoth bone met skull bone
                with a crack;
Joe was quick and precise in attack.
    With the death-blow delivered,
        The huge creature shivered,
And Joe quickly slid down its back.

For the long neck had started to sway.
That's when Joe tried a fast get-away.
The neck would soon fall,
Through the forest and all,
Demolishing trees on the way.

As the long neck was crashing through trees,
Joe was perched on its back, on his knees.
In a deafening thunder,
Poor Joe was sucked under
The water, which threatened to freeze.

Joe gurgled and thought he would die
But then on the shore he did spy
His Bo standing there,
This lady so fair;
To reach her, he surely must try.

She looked like a dream in disguise,
Her presence there was a surprise.
Hair flowed to her hips,
She had such luscious lips,
And a humorous glint in her eyes.

Joe struggled against the cold water.
His thoughts of the trophy he'd brought her
Renewed all his strength
And finally, at length,
He emerged, seeing God's perfect daughter.

He swam to the maid on the shore,
Triumphant, though soaked to the core.
He said, "See what I've brought you,
A present to court you.
What suitor could give you much more?"

She looked at the slain plessio,
Then turned her attention to Joe.
"Okay, clever-dick,
But tell me real quick,
How do I take home your large foe?"

Joe goggled and felt devastated.
His ego was rather deflated,
For he'd not given thought
To the mode of transport
For a creature so large and so weighted.

He roared in frustration, and charged
A nearby fruit tree, which he barged.
    A fruit, ripe and red,
    Fell straight on his head
Which only his daftness enlarged.

When Bo picked herself off the ground
And her laughter had echoed around.
    Joe wished she would stop,
    For he felt such a flop,
Feeling mortified, ruined and clowned.

But she then said, "My funny Joe sweet,
I'll never a braver man meet.
    And you make me laugh too,
    What more could man do
To make a cave-girl's life complete?"

Joe was the happiest cave-man in the world.

Jonah

Jonah was ate by a whale,
So we're told of this very sad tale.
While in the thing's tummy,
He played 'Royal Rummy'
And tried not to whimper or wail.

Julius' Rage

Julius Caesar was hurt
To notice his friends all desert.
But he hurt so much more,
When stabbed to the core,
He considered them all to be 'dirt'.

K

Kettle's Lament

There once was a shiny old kettle,
So proud of its coppery metal.
One day with a sigh,
It boiled itself dry,
And its black bum just stung like a nettle!

Katy Did Not

An eager young lady named Kate
Did get herself in quite a state,
'Cos she chatted up blokes
 With corny old jokes,
Then never turned up for a date.

Kay's Waywardness

A raunchy young lady named Kay
Just loved a good romp in the hay.
She used up the boys
As if they were toys
And now for her sins she must pay.

Ken's Pen

A terrible writer named Ken
Just thought himself greatest of men.
He wrote lots of stuff
That was not good enough.
He didn't have power to his pen.

Kit's Wit

There was a young lady called Kitty
Who thought herself terribly witty.
She was often quite sarky
Which made people narky.
She didn't deserve any pity.

Kong the Wronged

The infamous, massive King Kong
Really didn't do anything wrong —
Fell in love with a girl,
Thought she was a pearl,
They zapped him for being too strong.

Kookaburra Laughs

Kookaburra sits on a gum tree,
And laughs all the while, "Tee-hee-hee!"
He laughs till he drops
Enormous great plops.
Do tell us the joke, dear Kook-ee...

Tee-hee-hee-hee!

Lisa's Trip

There was a young lady called Lisa
Who suddenly fancied a pizza.
She ran to her car,
But didn't get far
Because she'd forgotten her keys – er!

Libra's Treat

Libra's the friendliest kind
With the sweetest smile you'll ever find.
    She likes people galore
    With a wide open door,
And adores to be oft' wined and dined.

Like It Was

As they boarded the Ark two by two,
Noah heartily welcomed his zoo.
    When their smells filled the air,
    Noah cried in despair,
"Every one of them needs a shampoo!"

Lisa's Folly

Another young lady called Lisa
She bought a brand spanking new freezer
    But the freezer got broke
    When she filled it with coke
And nothing you said could appease her.

Lawrie's Vacation

There was a young fellow named Lawrence
Whose holiday took him to Florence.
    He very soon found
    That he nearly got drowned,
'Cos the rain kept on falling in torrents.

Lil's Wardrobe

A terrible tomboy called Lily
Just couldn't stand anything frilly.
At all fancy clothes
She turned up her nose.
She thought them remarkably silly.

Leo Shines

Leo's a sign which is proud,
And sometimes quite vain and quite loud.
But the sunniest smile
On earth will beguile
Most people – and draw quite a crowd.

Liam's Relief

A young Irish fellow named Liam
Did visit a London museum.
Just inside the door
Stood a great dinosaur.
He said, "Jaysus! I'm glad they don't free 'em."

Liz's Duster

A dizzy young lady named Liz
Quite often got into a tizz.
Even got in a fluster
While stewing her duster,
And boiled over bright yellow fizz.

Lorraine's Marche

There was a poor French girl – Lorraine,
Who thought peasant clogs were mundane.
She longed for high heels
Just to know how it feels
To get your heel stuck in a drain.

M

Mary Had...

Mary, a little lamb had
And some people thought her
quite mad.
But Mary, undaunted,
At school her lamb flaunted,
Until it was cooked by
her Dad (*how sad*).

Macho Man Seeks Wife

The woman should not have a brain;
That makes her much harder to train.
But good she should look,
And know how to cook,
And from forming opinions, abstain.

Anonymous

Mark the Saint?

A kind-hearted fellow called Mark
Thought it might be a bit of a lark
To feed all the geese
With bread soaked in grease,
When he went for a walk in the park.

Mars Bar?

You've heard of the near planet Mars,
The reddest of our local stars,
Called 'Ares' in Greek,
'God of War' so to speak
But also makes fine chocolate bars.

Merlin's Error

That ancient magician called Merlin
Was always his magic unfurlin'.
One day, with a 'Zap!'
He turned gold to crap,
Which brought an onslaught of stones hurlin'.

Mike's Bike

A choosy young fellow named Michael
Just wanted a new mountain cycle.
He looked with dismay
At the massive display,
And said "How to decide when I like all?"

Mummy's 'Thank-You' Letter

In her thanks to a well-meaning shopper,
Mummy's note was exceedingly proper.
While the infant reposed,
Mummy smartly composed,
"Baby loves her electric corn-popper."
Anonymous

Myrt's Best Friend

A restless young woman named Myrtle
Decided the highways to hurtle.
She travelled the globe
In order to probe
But the best pal she found was a turtle.

Moth's Dismay

There was rather a zany young moft*
Whose brain was incredibly soft.
He flew into a light –
Got a terrible fright,
When both his antennae fell oft.

*'MOFT' = Cockney (*old London speak*) for 'MOTH'

N

Nanny's Lament

With babies I don't have much luck.
I feed them and then they upchuck
   And after each meal
   I then have to deal
 With the other end – Oh yucky-YUCK!

Neptune's Grace

Neptune (once known as Poseidon),
As 'sea god', could not be relied on.
If in a bad mood,
He would wreck ships (how rude!)
With mighty waves surfers could ride on.

Neville's Pact

There was a young fellow called Neville
Who sold his own soul to the devil.
He had a great life
And a fabulous wife
Then died and accepted his level.

Nicky's Knack

There was a young person called Nicky
Who was known to be terribly picky.
She tried all her might
To do things that were right,
But everyone just took the mickey.

Norman's Obligation

A naïve young fellow called Norman,
Quite fancied himself as a doorman.
He clocked in his mates,
Regardless of dates
Then had to explain to the foreman.

Nymph, Nymph...

A nymph with a string of glass beads
Was hailed by a goblin in tweeds.
He said, "They're not real jewels,
Green glass is for fools!"
She said, "Bugger off back to your reeds!"

Apology to Harold Monro

Naomi at Home

Such a very sweet girl was Naomi,
She loved everything that was homey.
She watched lots of telly
And made apple jelly
Then soaked in a bath that was foamy.

Oliver's Spurning

An amorous fellow named Ollie
Fell in love with a beautiful dolly
But she sniffed with disdain
At his wooing in vain;
She thought he was rather a wally.

Octavia's Rule

The very posh Lady, Octavia
Just cannot stand uncouth behaviour.
If you were to swear
At the time she was there
Then nothing on this earth could save yer.

Oki

A beautiful owl name of Oki
One day got decidedly croaky.
He croaked and he spluttered
Then vehemently muttered,
' It's the fault of those humans so smoky'.

Opportunity

A dim-witted fellow named Sly,
While at the Post-Office did spy:
"WANTED: Bank Robber"
Thought, "I'm an odd-jobber,"
Then asked for a form to apply.

Anonymous

Orion the Hunter

The great constellation Orion
With heart just as brave as a lion,
Is stuck up in the sky
With nothing to spy
Except Earth, which he keeps a good eye on.

Out of Tune

When Nero attempted to sing
While plucking his harp, ting-a-ling,
The long-suff'ring Romans
All prayed for good omens
To stifle the noise of that thing.

Owen's Good Intentions

There was a young fellow named Owen
Who dreamed about hoein' and mowin';
Yet he spent summer days
In his deckchair to laze
And just watched the weeds all a-growin'.

Owl v Cat

An owl and a fat pussy-cat
Were adrift on a boat. Fancy that!
When they'd finished the cheese,
With instinctive unease,
They thought they would share the last rat.

We think Edward would approve

P

Paul the Short

A rather short fellow named Paul
Just longed to be terribly tall
So he went to the pub
And ate lots of grub
But still he remained very small.

Pearl Drops

A rather wet lady named Pearl
Whose brolly just wouldn't unfurl,
Just struggled and strained
The whole time it rained
And ended up pooled in a whirl.

Penny Bright

A certain Penelope Hinton
Admired anything with a glint on.
So she polished her car
'Til it shone like a star,
Then didn't dare lay a thumbprint on.

Peter the Poet

There was a young poet called Peter
Whose writings just couldn't be neater.
He wrote every word
Like the song of a bird,
And no-one could pen a verse sweeter.

Pilchard's Pain

An unhappy pilchard called Nellie
Had quite a bad pain in the belly,
So she drank castor oil
Which was quite near the boil,
Then turned into strawberry jelly.

Pluto and Persephone

Pluto, the ruler of Hades,
Did not have much luck with the ladies,
So he kidnapped a belle,
Whisked her off down to Hell,
Till he tired of her mother's fierce raidies.

Polygamy, the Downside

When reading the bible, I saw
In Solomon's Book, a great flaw:
Even though every wife
Brought much joy to his life,
Each came with a mother-in-law.
Anonymous

Pure and Simple

A pumice stone's good for your feet,
And a nail brush is quite hard to beat
But a face washed with soap
(the mild sort, we hope)
Will ensure your complexion is sweet.

Pyromaniac

A fellow equipped with a biro
Once forged someone's sig. on a giro.
Then he burned evi-dence
Of his gross fraudulence.
His crime turned him into a 'pyro'.

Pisces the Susser

The gentl-est sign of all time,
Pisces loves just to paint and to rhyme.
Though sometimes unruly,
It's usually 'cos newly
Creating some thing that's sublime.

Q

Quasi Modo

A hunchback from old Notre Dame
Quite accepted his own lack of charm.
As he tolled his great bell,
He thought, "What the hell?
I'm fine as I am, thank you Ma'am."

Quiche Lorraine

Take a pastry case bought from a store.
Fill with onions, cheese, mushrooms galore,
Then with eggs that are beaten,
Chives, garlic to sweeten
And bake at gas mark 5 or 4.

Quorn

Quorn is an edible fungus
With nutrient value humungus.
You can buy it in chunks,
Or minced, or great hunks.
What a blessing that Nature has brung us

Quack Tactics

There once was a rather daft quack
Who thought he would try a new tack.
He prescribed all his patients
Some pills that were ancient
And most of them never came back.

Quasar, Quasar..

A quasar's not really a star.
We're blowed if we know what they are.
But signals we hear
With detection-type gear.
And light pulses sent from afar.

Queenie's Dosh

There was a young lady called Queenie
Who was known to be rather a meanie.
She counted each cent
With concern rever-ent,
But her bank account still remained teeny.

R

Rapunzel (*Another Limsaga*)

Fair Rapunzel was locked in a tower,
Growing sadder each day by the hour,
Till one morning she found
That her hair reached the ground,
"What a bummer!" she thought with a glower.

A handsome prince came riding by.
He saw this gold fall from the sky.
He looked up and spied
The princess who cried
In her tower – so wretchedly high.

He heard her most mournful boo-hoo,
And quickly saw what he must do;
He said, "Ma cherie,
I'll soon have you free."
Then off of his stallion he flew.

He called up to the maiden so fair,
"You have truly magnificent hair.
Would you mind awful-ly
If I climbed up to thee
With these tresses to use as my stair?"

"Oh, Dear Prince, I do not mind at all;
I will anchor myself to the wall
    With the coat-hooks thereon.
        See, my nerve is not gone.
Please be careful that you do not fall."

Thus welcomed, he started to climb
Up onto those tresses sublime.

He worried at first
Quite fearing the worst;
To hurt her would be
            such a crime.

At last he arrived in her cell,
Her misery set to dispel.
She said, "Well, my pet,
I don't wish to fret,
But now you are up here as well."

He said, "Don't you worry, my dear;
The answer is perfectly clear.
I'll hold onto your hair
With the greatest of care,
And lower you straight down from here."

He did so with manly aplomb;
A happy lass she had become.
When she got to the ground
The big stallion she found,
Who wondered where she had come from.

The Prince called her name from the tower,
"Rapunzel, my beautiful flower,
   Just throw up your hair
   So lustrous and fair,
I'll be with you inside the hour."

She laughed at that foolish Don Juan;
The Prince was a stupid mor-on.
      For you cannot throw hair
            Fifty feet in the air...
She just mounted the horse – and was gone.

Reggie's Lament

A certain Sir Reginald Proctor
Developed a bad case of lockjaw.
He picked up the phone
And started to moan
But couldn't get through to the doctor.

Reading Ragamuffin

There was a young lady from Reading
Whose new shoes were 'doing her head in'.
She stepped on a lace
And fell flat on her face.
She should've looked where she was treading.

Red Riding Hood's Rage

When he saw her bright cloak in the wood,
A wolf thought it would be quite good
To swallow the Granny,
Then if he was canny,
He'd still get the girl and the food.

But 'Riding Hood' wasn't impressed.
She saw he was just a wolf dressed.
With her basket of shopping,
She gave Wolf a whopping,
And broke eggs all over his vest.

Rich Ointment

A fussy young fellow named Richie
Had ears that kept going all twitchy;
So he gave them a rub
With some stuff in a tub;
And then they went red and all itchy.

Rosie Cozy

There was a young lady called Rosie
Who loved to be snug, warm and cozy.
If the weather was cold,
She would not be cajolled;
She just stayed in bed nice and dozy.

Ruthless

A very shrewd lady named Ruth
Had ambition to be a great sleuth.
She dazzled her clients
With snippets of science
And often embroidered the truth.

Ryvita

All slimmers hate bread made from rye.
"Why can't we have real bread?" they cry.
With lettuce and stuff
It is never enough.
It's also quite brittle and dry.

Rudolph

Rudolph the Reindeer of old
Had a nose that went red in the cold.
Though everyone laughed
And thought he looked daft,
His story is constantly told.

S

Sam Sticky

A cute little baby called Sam
Just loved eating strawberry jam
But found it quite tricky
When he was all sticky,
And got rather glued to his pram.

Sagittarius Free

The Zodiac's wildest, wild child,
Yet, the wittiest, and the most smiled.
Saggy has heights
And stars in his sights,
And is not the most easily riled.

Santa the Merry

Such a merry old fellow was Santa,
So fond of the Christmassy banter.
He said "Ho Ho Ho!"
And "Yipee-i-oh!"
And the reindeer took off at a canter.

Saturn the Meanie

Saturn is famed for its rings,
All sparkly with diamonds and things.
Yet it seems so unfair
That they're stuck way up there,
Out of reach – if you even had wings.

Scorpio's Secret

Scorpio's deepest of all.
Life for him is not much of a ball.
For he hides everything
Which other folks sing.
Only courage can break down his wall.

S'now Joke

A very fine snowman called Joe
Forgot he was made out of snow.
He had a hot drink
While he sat in the sink
Then straight down the plug-hole did go.

Stevie Wonder

There was a young fellow named Steve
Whose cheek you just wouldn't believe.
He walked in the pub,
Said, "Give us a sub"
And a free pint of beer did receive.

Sue's Education

There was a young lady called Sue
Who didn't have much of a clue.
She went back to college
To catch up her knowledge,
And ended up catching the flu'.

Sweet Talk

My favourite sweetener is honey.
I like the thick kind, not the runny.
I spread it on peas,
Bananas and cheese.
Do you think that my taste buds are funny?

Squirrels

The reds have gone north
of the Border.
We really think that's out of order.

We're stuck
with the greys
Till the end of our days
Who don't look so bright on camcorder.

T

Taurus' Territory

Taurus likes life to be good
With masses of comfort and food.
The armchair's his throne,
With computer and phone;
He'd rule the whole world if he could.

Tam the Clam

There was a young lady called Tammy
Whose hands were incredibly clammy.
Though she washed them a lot,
She was always so hot,
They still felt all sticky and jammy.

Terri's Ruin

There was a young lady named Terri
Who was quite fond of hitting the sherry.
A job interview,
She never got through,
Because she was always too merry.

Thor's Tantrum

An old ancient god known as Thor
Was known to chuck thunder and roar.
He did this one night
While the earth quaked in fright;
Then they learned to build lightning rods more.

Tom, Tom

Thomas, that old piper's son
Ran off with a pig he had won
But the poor pig was nicked
And its bones duly picked,
So pork chops, poor Tommy got none.

Tony the Rake

There was a young fellow called Tony
Who was very unnaturally bony.
Though he padded his clothes
And attempted to pose,
The ladies all knew he was phoney.

Tutankhamen

An Egyptian king once known as 'Tut'
In his life was not more than a mutt.
But he died very young,
And to Egypt he brung
Some curses and also some gut.

Twisted Justice

A poor child called Oliver Twist
Was known to have mother-love missed.
When he asked for more gruel,
He was banished from school.
To a master both wicked and pissed.

Trevor Unclever

There was an old fellow named Trevor
Who really was not very clever.
He did all his sums
With the stones out of plums,
And books he just couldn't read ever.

U

Ulysses

Ulysses, sailor so bold
Was cursed by a witch
(so we're told).

His fate was to roam
Twenty years on the foam.

By the time he got home, he was old.

Uke the Fluke

Uke was a fine unicorn
So proud of his spirally horn,
Till he met a young mare
Who thought him a scare
And neighed on a hilltop at dawn.

Upgraded

"Upon a time once" it was said
All good stories began that we read
But these days we find
No-one bears that in mind.
It's more like, "When I was last dead..."

Uranus

Uranus, the planet bizarre
Is the weirdest in System So-lar.
It rotates on its back,
Disregarding the pack.
What a nice unconventional star!

Usher Extraordinaire

An 'over the top' kind of usher
Was known to be rather a gusher.
He swamped all his guests
With flattering jests;
He just couldn't get any lusher.

Uther the Bad

There once was an old king called Uther
Who couldn't have been more uncouther.
He gambled and swore
And had rum deals galore.
His rival was only Lex Luther.

Una's Fancy

A young Scottish lassie called Una
Had rather a weakness for tuna.
She scoffed by the tinful,
Although it was sinful
She just couldn't get enough doon her.

V

Vic's New career

A resourceful young fellow named Vic
Was only just out of the nick.
He decided to bake
For his fortune to make;
But sadly, his cake tins did stick.

Val the Pal

There was a young lady called Val
Who was such a nice kind of gal.
She treated her friends
With presents and lends;
She was the ideal kind of pal.

Venus Rising

Venus, the bright morning star,
Clearly shows sailing ships where they are.
So the Ancients agree
That she rose from the sea.
Now we think that's a little fetched-far.

Vera the Jeerer

A rather unkind girl named Vera
Just was an incurable jeerer.
Her pranks were designed
Folks' raw spot to find.
It couldn't have been any clearer.

Virgo's Devotion

Virgo's the fussiest type,
Reputed to moan and to gripe.
But it's not always true,
Dedicated to you,
She will bring you your slippers and pipe.

Voltaire

Francois was a very French writer
Who turned out to be quite a fighter.
He wrote lots of jokes
And poked fun at some folks.
There were many who thought him a blighter.

Vulcan

A heavenly blacksmith of yore,
Forged weapons for Mars (god of war),
But 'Trekkies' imply
That Vulcans are high
On the list of the 'peacemaking' corps.

Anonymous

Viv's Lesson

There was a young teacher named Viv
Who cookery lessons did give.
But his talents were few
When making a roux;
He said, 'Put everything through a sieve.'

W

Wayne's Regret

A lazy young fellow called Wayne
Took a walk down a long country lane.
The sun it was baking,
His feet started aching;
He wished he had taken the train.

Wendy, Trendsetter

There was a young lady named Wendy
Who really was not very trendy.
She bought some tight trews
Which were very bad news,
As her legs were too thin and quite bendy.

Whale of a Time

There once was a silly old whale
Who thought his complexion too pale
So he leapt round a pool
Till he felt quite a fool
Then blushed from his nose to his tail.

Win's Run

The unfortunate Winnie the Pooh
Just didn't quite know what to do.
He ate loads of honey,
Which was rather runny
And spent the whole night on the loo.

Wizard Recipe

There was a not very wise Wizard
Who thought he would dine on a lizard.
Though he stewed it in brine
And plenty of wine
It ended up stuck in his gizzard.

Woden's Day

A 'Scandy' old god name of Woden
Delighted in earthly types goadin'.
He gave them midweek
For his blessing to seek,
Then declared that weekends were *verboten*.

Wombatiquette

If you're ever scared by a wombat,
There's no need for heavy armed combat.
Just dig a big hole,
Then go like a mole.
He's a really not out of hell from bat.

X

Xantheneous

There's a bright lurid dye called Xanthene
Which is in between yellow and green.
It's likely to dazzle
And cause nerves to frazzle
Yet plain in the dark can be seen.

XI

Consider the Roman 'eleven'
Or a fine football side up from Devon.
For kids it means 'plus';
Open pub time for us
And Apostles when Judas skipped Heaven.

X

X is a very fine letter;
It's a challenge to find one that's better.
It *can* mean a kiss,
Roman ten, or beat this...
When unknown, it's a tempting 'go-getter'.

Xanthippe

A nagging wife, name of Xanthippe
Was known to be terribly lippy.
She gave Socrates hell,
Which was just as well
He chose to end life as a Hippie.

Xaving Grace

A very just man called St. Xaviour
Was known for his righteous behaviour.
He did all he could
To be very good,
And blessings he willingly gave yer.

X-Clusive

The elusive and strange Planet X
Is said to bemuse and perplex.
Though widely renowned,
It has never been found,
Thus surely a reason to vex.

Xerxes

An old Persian ruler named Xerxes
Was known for his maddening quirkses.

He sent ele-phants

And the Greeks wet their pants,
Which made them feel somewhat like burkses.

Y

Yellow Paws

A young pussy-cat who was yellow,
Decided it would be more mellow
To dye her fur grey
And maybe that way
She'd land her a handsome tom fellow.

Yakety-Yak

There once was a hairy old yak
Who strayed from the well-beaten track.
When he asked a big bird
The way back to the herd,
It said, "Dunno, 'cos I'm all right Jack."

Yip-Yap

Puppies will Yap or say 'Yip'
And will bite everything they can nip.
But they'll puddle the floor
If you shout, rage and roar.
They're cutest of all when a-kip.

Yokel's Demise

A rather uncouth country yokel
Went for a quick pint in his local.
Unfortunate-ly
He drank twenty-three
And became uncommonly vocal.

Yorkshire Wails

The not-so-grand Duke of old York
Was fed up with having to walk.
He was tired of long drills
And marching up hills,
So went on vacation to Cork.

Yule Log

The festive occasion of Yule
(Or so I was taught back in school)
Was here long before
Christianity's Law,
But choccie logs still make me drool.

Yvette's Brew

There was a young lady, Yvette
Who was rather inclined to forget.
One day she forgot
To put tea in the pot,
So sugary water did get.

Z

Zack the Black

There was a young fellow named Zack
Who insisted on wearing just black.

One dark foggy night,
He went quite out of sight
And never did find his way back.

Zander's Leap

A dafter-than-average old zander
To mankind had no wish to pander
So jumped from the river
With fins all a-quiver –
Became an inpromptu bank lander.

Zena's Beans

There was a young lady named Zena
Who wanted the world to be greener.
She planted some seeds
Too big for her needs
And no-one has since ever seen her.

Zeusology

The king of Olympus was Zeus.
In his heaven he hurled out abuse.
He crushed other gods
'Cos he thought they were sods,
But with people he ordered a truce.

Zirconia

Zirconia's a diamond that's made
With the efforts of men in the trade.
It's not to be knocked;
Many people have flocked
To buy one, without being dismayed.

Zoe Cool

A nice little girl name of Zoe
Was excited to find it was snowy.
She ran out to play
And stayed there all day
Till her fingers and toes got all glowy.

Zorro's Owings

There once was a cowboy called Zorro,
So broke he was tempted to borrow.
He placed a few bets
Just to clear up his debts
Then lost all his dosh – to his sorrow.

Printed in the USA
CPSIA information can be obtained
at www.ICGtesting.com
LVHW071732171023
761361LV00001B/4